World Stage Press

Verse from the Village

My AfroRican State of Soul

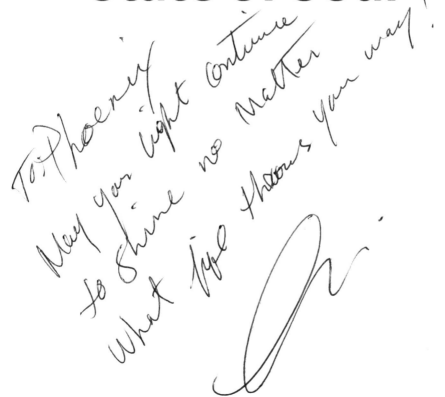

To: Phoenix

May your light continue
to shine no matter
what type throws your way!

My AfroRican State of Soul
A Journey of Identidad, Struggle, Love & Faith

Lucas Rivera

World Stage Press
Verse from the Village

World Stage Press
Verse from the Village

My AfroRican State of Soul
© 2023 Lucas Rivera
ISBN: 978-1-952952-55-5

First Edition, 2023

Printed in the United States of America

Edited by Valentina Gomez & Ruddy Lopez
Cover Design by Lucas Rivera & Emily Anne Evans
Cover Photograph by Lucas Rivera
Layout Design by Emily Anne Evans

I dedicate this book to my family. Rubi, my beuutiful wife, friend, and first real love. To my two boys, Lil' Lucas and Kahlo, who remind me each day to be the best father and man I can possibly be. To my mother who sacrificed it all to raise me and my four brothers alone. To my brothers who I shared the best and worst moments of my adolescent life with. To my father, whose absence allowed me to be a real dad, husband, and positive role model to my children.

Finally, to the reader, who I hope this book can inspire to find love in all the creations of God.

Contents

Love

Faith

Foreword

Ruha Benjamin
Professor of African American Studies, Princeton University

All aboard this sonic ship, fueled by tenderness, guided by faith, and grounded by the boom bap of ancestral beats. Wordsmith extraordinaire Lucas Rivera steers us through treacherous terrain. Unencumbered by spacetime, we travel to childhoods in Puerto Rico, South Bronx, and North Philly, and propel towards futures electrified by visions of justice and joy. The soundtrack of this ship is love.

Around every corner we can hear echoes of passengers past. Verses that grow "wings greater than walls," like Sun Ra, odes that call out to us, "*Caminante, no hay puentes. Se hacen puentes al andar,*" a la Gloria Anzaldúa,[1] and lyrics that swagger "through jeering streets," like the best of Robert Hayden. Some say this ship is haunted. I say that spiritual giants are accompanying us on the journey — their fingerprints lining each page, their pride beaming down on this beautiful Boricua poet steering us closer to ourselves.

To be sure, it is not just where we go, but *how* we go on this journey. We are hip to the baggage we carry from generations past — what the experts call "intergenerational trauma." But Rivera invites us to witness intergenerational *healing*. His poetry not only names the pain — "the trauma *mamá* endured by *papá's* addiction" — but also illuminates the potential: "He begins to create a new language/ Living life/ Playing the body like an instrument/ Letting go." Letting go and traveling lighter.

Healing, after all, cannot be conjured by new policies and laws, but can only emerge from a new poetics — creative care and attention to how we treat and value one another. *Poiesis*: to bring something into being that did not exist before. Like a young child who longs for his absent father, metabolizing his grief and rage, until finally he becomes an extraordinary father that did not exist before. *Cardiopoeisis*: the potential to regenerate new heart cells. Biologists are just figuring out what the poets have always known — that each of us is a creator; creating ourselves by recreating our world. The compass for this journey is the Creative Word.

Prepare to be transported.

---

[1] Translation: Voyager, there are no bridges, one builds them as one walks.

My AfroRican State of Soul

A Journey of Identidad, Struggle, Love & Faith

Identidad

Identidad for me is defined as the culture, and the history of that culture reflected in our own selves, which makes us uniquely beautiful. It is not a look, but a state of being, acting, and presenting self in the world through language, food, art, music, dance, faith. It is shaped by the understanding of our past, guided by an individual relationship with God, and grounded by our hopes for the future of mankind.

I once did not know who I was. I felt like I had no purpose — no goals. My desires and hopes had not been formulated yet, and, simply stated, I was a hot mess. In the summer of 1992, I was introduced to a special place: Taller Puertorriqueño. A cultural arts center in the heart of North Philadelphia, dedicated to the education and preservation of our Latino history through art, literature, and music. It was there that I was introduced to who I was as an Afro-Rican (a Puerto Rican who self-identifies as Black). It was there that I began to love myself for who I was, how I looked, and how I spoke. It was there that I learned about the injustices our *Isla* of Puerto Rico endured for centuries. It was at Taller that I began to embrace my *cultura*, which is reflected in my music, my art, my dance, and poetry. In this process of understanding the self through culture, I began to move closer to God without even knowing it.

"In The Beginning" Prelude

I was born on Thursday, December 29, 1977, in a small *barrio* in the city of Salinas, Puerto Rico. I was named after my father, so technically that makes me a Jr., although I never use it. I was my father's first son and my mother's third. Yes, she hooked up with *papá* after having two children from previous relationships in the South Bronx, New York. After the death of her second husband, she flew back home to Puerto Rico and met my father. She told me stories about his beautiful smile and how he didn't care that she had kids. She said that *papá* fell in love with her pretty fast, as she did with him. That was truly my beginning.

We first lived with *papá's* mother, who didn't really have any care for *mamá*. She believed it was because she had two kids when getting together with *papá*. In those days that type of relationship was frowned upon. Despite it all, *mamá* and *papá* had me and two more children. They finally got their own place, and we lived there until I was about five years old. Our home, as described by *mamá*, wasn't too big. However, *papá* gave us everything we needed. She said that he also loved my two older brothers as if they were his. We were happy there and created many memories. Some good, some not so good.

Mamá met *papá* soon after he was drafted to fight in Vietnam. He would come home for breaks for a few months at a time. That's when he would drink with his friends and experiment with other drugs until he got hooked. It got worse as time went by. The last few times he would come home he would get so drunk and become very abusive towards *mamá*. It got so bad that one day during his last deployment, *mamá* took us all and headed to the Bronx on a one-way flight she got her aunt to purchase. We landed in the Bronx with little to nothing. She didn't have much to her name, but she started a new life for us — her and her five boys — in the big city she knew so well.

I don't remember much about my birthplace, but I get emotional every time I land at the airport in San Juan when I visit. It's almost like *la Isla* hugs me so tight that I can't help but get choked up and filled with joy. I have countless dreams about *mi Isla*. In my dreams I can smell the scent of mango trees and passion fruit, and even hear the beautiful sound of the *coquí* at night. We lived in a small shack-style house that leaked every time it rained. Pots surrounded the living room, and my job was to make sure the pots didn't overfill with rainwater. Our front and back yards were huge. We had almost an acre of land — mostly dirt with some small palm trees that fruited coconuts. We also had a mango tree and a quenepa tree in the back of the house, and a tall avocado tree in the front. *Papá* had a huge pig tied to that avocado tree that was too fat to even stand up. I used to call her *Flaca*. We also had chickens, twelve of *Flaca*'s piglets, and a goat. *Mi* Puerto Rico is, and will always continues to be, my home. Whether in my dreams or in the fragments of my childhood memories, it is dear to me — as if a part of me has been left behind with her. Every day I long to sink my feet in her white sands and smell the sweetness of her fruit trees.

In the Beginning

In the beginning,
At least the beginning of my beginning,
Although I came in the middle of this story,
Sitting at the center of two brothers that came before,
And two that came after.

I stand,

Pulled by dreams that never came,
And hope that someday may change our outcome.
That's where it all began,
And I, for years after, struggled to find who I am.

One of five individual spirits
Curated by one light.
A light dimming in a journey of heartbreak and struggle,
And I, for years after, wondered where I fit in.

Coming to terms as if it was already destined for me.

I breathe.

Inhale the dilemma at hand —
A band with five lead singers,
An inexperienced manager,
No lights,
No sound,
No stage.

Mamá, who did the best she could,
At the edge of fight or flight,

And three baby daddies, with the last one at war with addiction —
Never taking responsibility but convincing *mamá* he would

And that's where *papá* stood, and that's where I stand.
Exhale in order to find my place in this space,
On this stage,
This song was already written a long time ago.

I stand.

Inhale the scent of mango trees.
La Isla del Encanto,
Mi tierra,
The land that held my spirit.
My feet grounded in the beginning of my dreams,
Our fears,
Her escape.

We gave her life, she said,
But it was her that saved ours.
We stood.

Five lead singers of one band,

And I the center and beginning of the new verse,
Exhale the one note that pivots a narrative told many years ago.

Inhale the trauma *mamá* endured by *papá's* addiction,
Afflicting pain so deep in her composition
It made *boleros* sound like a carnival.

Heart broken,
And its broken pieces torn,

And its torn essence,
Crushed, made to dust that she thought was love.

And my beginning comes after.
The third of five,
The center,
And throughout my life I grappled to center self.

I close my eyes and remember the scent of *la Isla*
As if I was still standing in its *Yunque.*
The sound of the *coquí,*
The majestic melody of its indigenous opera.

Mamá truly felt as if life was giving her a third chance,
Greeting *papá* at the door as he returned from war,
Soon realizing that the war never returned *papá.*

In the beginning,
At least the beginning of my beginning,
Her third hope.
Instead, she endured the pain and suffering of a new man's trauma.
It was her that saved us.

Mamá thought it was the beginning of new dreams brought to light —
Dreams realized by promises fading in clear sight.
She thought this now new man, dream, would stay a little longer.
Linger and manifest happier days.

I remember the last time *papá* went away.
Fleeing it all, she packed her lead singers
And took us on tour.
One-way trip to the States — she wrote our next song.

Birth of a Dancer

A child is born
In full contact with life
At the first touch of earth
His body begins to move

In the beginning there was a force —
A force that made his body move
And although his head is heavy
He can feel a rhythm that takes over

The dance continues in silence —
A graceful silence —
A dance moving like silk riding the wind
He begins

His language is movement
The dance of a child
A child who only speaks with his
Hips
Arms
Head
And feet

Now in full contact with life
And in this life cycle there is peace
A peace within the body
Mind
Soul

Knowing no wrong
Only love

Knowing no fear
Only the desire to move to the internal sound

He begins to create a new language
Living life
Playing the body like an instrument
Letting go
Releasing all through his dance

Listening
Being aware of land
Soil
Mother Earth is his stage

Being aware of land
Of the creatures that dance with him
Of the element called contact
And the sound called *Cultura*
And the dance called Love

Sin Clave no hay Rumba

Sin Clave no hay Rumba
Sin Clave no hay Rumba

my heart beats like a drum
a rhythm that rises like the sun
a percussive sound
first found
in the womb of *mamá*
in the womb of *mamá*

this rhythm is a calling
a calling by our ancestors

a calling through *Rumba*
that awakens the cells
reminding you of our Blackness
mistaken by others as less than

this *clave* is the foundation
of all that came before
and all who will come after

Sin Clave no hay Rumba
Sin Clave no hay Rumba

this rhythm cannot be ignored
it cannot be sampled
it is the DNA of our soul
the first note we played
when we engaged
with Mother Earth
the first

Sin Clave no hay Rumba
Sin Clave no hay Rumba

can you feel the drum
pulsating inside our minds

running through the *sangre* in our veins
let's create space and engage
navigating the dance floor with open heart
mind clear
arms out in full embrace

responding to the musicality
the richness of our *cultura*
the roots of our *identidad*
the sound we all sang
when they took us from our land
when they took us from our land

Sin Clave no hay Rumba
Sin Clave no hay Rumba

Now that we are all here
unidad, cultura
one circle, one sphere
creating a new sound
clave and house kicks
so no one sits down
this is our sound
bound and renowned

Sin Clave no hay Rumba
Sin Clave no hay Rumba

Soy Afro-Boricua

I am the child of weeping *Taína* queens
African slaves who gave them comfort
Soy el color of blended love
El Afro-Boricua from a sacred land
Una Isla forgotten and those that came before us now gone

Soy Afro-Boricua
Mixed with the blood of *mamá* Africa
Taíno Indians native to the land
I'm the child of beautiful melanin skin
The reflection of truth to untold stories of our deep roots

A child of *una Isla rica* — *playas* of clear blue water and white sand
Una Isla invaded by so-called Spanish explorers
But *Conquistadores* they were who no longer stand
And although I've tried to denounce it
That Spanish blood also runs deep through my chest

Tall and proud of his roots *el negrito* screams — *¡¡¡LIBERTAD!!!*
I am Afro-Boricua
I am

Dark brown eyes filled with the love and pain turned tears of his people

Head crowned with locs reflecting the masses bounded together as one

Chest lifted towards the sun soaking in the Creator's light
Feet standing on ancestral ground
Blessed by their prayers for a better day
A Freedom Day

I am, Afro-Boricua I am

Hope

Aquí llegué - Aquí llegué
They chanted holding hands as, one by one, they exit the plane
And touch, for the first time the land of the free

Aquí llegué
America
Aquí llegué
And again
Aquí llegué

Have you ever witnessed five hundred Boricua hands clapping
after safely landing on the tarmac in America?

Hoping
Traveling from *la Isla* on large airbuses

One-way promises
Promises of a better life in the Big Apple
But ending up in sweat shops
Stitching together a life torn apart

Chanting as they worked
Boricua *hermanas y madres*
Chanting together as they worked
Aquí llegué - Aquí llegué

Hope
Hoping for a better life
Cashing in on agreements by politics
With rubber checks

Trying to stay hydrated while
Their heated bodies squeeze out that last drip
Drip of hydration, the last drop
In the sweat shop

Where machines —
No, their hands —
Their bare hands —
blistering hands push to hit the daily garment quota

Boricuas on the production line ready to clock out
Hands, feet, back
Their beaten bodies can't wait to clock out
Mamá's working a double

Hope
Hoping for a better day
And at midnight when she finally gets in
I can hear her cry
Chanting

Aquí llegué
Pero por qué
Por qué
Por qué

Morning rises, but we speak not
Searching for a better life
Hoping for a better life
They landed in America alone

Young women leaving all they had back home
Hoping for a better life
En los Estados Un-i-dos
Yeah, right

Chanting
Holding on to identity
Cultura, idioma
Chanting

Aquí llegué
Aquí llegué
Pero por qué

Corazón Negro

Mi corazón de sangre negra
Enterrado en la tierra de mi madre

Mis ojos de color canela
Reflejan la historia de la esclavitud que nunca olvidaremos

Piel dura y oscura como la cáscara del coco
Un recuerdo de la naturaleza que me robaron

Y mi cabello de trenzas negras
Una fuerza que jamás podrás vencer

Nuestra tierra reclamada
Por el espíritu de nuestro corazón negro

Semilla por semilla
Las manos de mi gente reconstruirán

Dejando las huellas de una generación libre
Que nos garantizan un futuro de esperanza

Mi corazón de sangre negra
Enterrado en la tierra de mi madre

Y tu verdadera mirada de ladrón
Disfrazado en piel de amigo

Te dejo en tu conciencia
Las cenizas de nuestros ancestros

Para que torturen tus pesadillas
Y nunca olvides el genocidio de Mi Pueblo

Corazón Negro

My black-blooded heart
Buried in my mother's land

Light brown eyes
Reflecting a history of slavery that I will never forget

My skin, dark and strong like a coconut shell
A memory of the pure essence that you stole from me

And my black, braided hair
A force that can never be broken

The spirits of my peoples' black hearts
Reclaimed this land

And seed by seed
Their hands will rebuild

Leaving the traces of a free generation
That will guarantee us a future of hope

My black-blooded heart
Buried in my mother's land

Your true thieving identity
Disguised in the skin of a friend

I leave in your conscience
The ashes of my ancestors

So that you remember them in your nightmares
And never forget the genocide of My People

We Rocked in The South Bronx

The South Bronx was home to my electric boogie
Head spins and footwork was my newfound idiom
And weekends at the courtyard made Carnegie Hall concerts
feel like opening acts

And my hat
was always turned to the side
profiling the fresh stripes on my shell tops

We rocked at the height of hip-hop
Beats laced with conga slaps
El clave, the foundation of our Latin sound
bridging the Black-Brown gap
Boricua, Morena, that was my *barrio*'s soundtrack

And at every block party
you can hear *mamá* throwing down on *Mi Viejo San Juan*
Sounds of salsa reverberating off apartment buildings
set off the soundtrack to our lullabies
Those were the days

On Sundays you would catch us smacking on penny candy
from the corner bodega
The owner, Luz, would give us cash for the empty beer cans we collected
From the old heads who partied the night before
Clapping hands, beating drums, and freestyling songs

And on Monday we couldn't wait for the week to end
Tony, Carlito, Jay Jay, and I would do it again
Bragging about being on the Rock Steady Crew
But no one knew that what bonded us all was the sound of the Bronx

That rumba-turned-salsa remixed into hip-hop
True birthplace of the head pop
Music that lifted our people up
Standing united *en mi barrio,*
The South Bronx, The South South Bronx

From Young Lords to Black Panthers
I wish you could have been there back then
I wish you could have been there back when
When Hip-Hop, BeBop, and Salsa were all friends

Aquí Llegó El Bembé

I grew up in conga-filled house parties
Mamá singing *boleros*
Cause this
was the sound of my ghetto

Shekere syncopated shells
Clapping in perfect motion
This was the sound of *mi barrio*
A chant filling the night

The elders sipping their night
The young fighting their fight
The sound creeping
Tricking you that it was still daylight

And the stars dancing
While the moon smiles his last smile
And the sun waiting in line
And the young mesmerized
By the beats of the drum

Aquí llegó
El bembé llegó
Aquí llegó
Aquí llegó
El bembé llegó

I grew up in conga slap homes
Today, *mi casa*
Tomorrow, my *tití*'s home
And the elders danced

Have you ever seen them dance
How the older men flow
How, without a word,
A motion from left to right unfolds,
bold and untold
yo

That old head is dope
And this *bembé* yo
This right here yo
This is the motherland
Reminding us who we are

Aquí llegó
El bembé llegó
Aquí llegó
Aquí llegó
El bembé llegó

I grew up *en el barrio*
Where police sirens were filtered out
By house parties
By *"Le-Lo-Lai"* and cuatros strumming nightly

The soundtrack of my hood
Aquí lo que hay es rumba
and that's where I stood

If you listen closely you can hear them calling
If we silence our distractions you can hear them calling
If we open our hearts we can all respond

And night after night we can all sing the same song

Aquí llegó
El bembé llegó
Aquí llegó
Aquí llegó
El bembé llegó

Cosmic Dancer

We are the dancers of the universe
We are its stars and its many moons

Illuminating the night sky
We move in the infinite multiverse

In syncopation with the sounds of comets,
Black holes, and meteor showers

Our bodies take over the dance floor
Our souls lost in Afro-beats and kick drums
Nubians the nu-being in new and old worlds

Melodies that melodically transform
Our spaces in warp speed
We move through multi-dimensions

Extensions of our limbs dancing in spaces
Unseen but felt deep in our veins
The blame for our heart's rhythmic bliss

A moment of out-of-body experiences
We are the dancers of our own internal sounds

The silence in our souls dropping the first beat
We dance to internal sound clouds
Everlasting waves powering the one source

Heart beats to sixteen notes
Legato scales keep us centered on our melodic journeys
Reconnecting the humanity
Grounded firmly

The me

The you

This land

This verse

Dancing in the light of one Sun.

A Puerto Rican Proclamation

Oye la ahí, la tierra está llamando

We are reclaiming *la tierra*
So goodbye oppressors
Go
Take your ignorance with you

This *tierra* belongs to us
A tribe grounded in the ways of this land
And with these hands
We Reclaim

Montañas and Valleys
Palmas and gardens of *esperanza*
Infinite miles of cultivated perfection
The sustenance that blesses our children

A new generation of warriors
Standing at the frontline with their javelins of poetry
Spittin' stanzas that unite *un pueblo*
Contra la destrucción of our land

Intone our *gente* chants
A call and response with *madre tierra*

Oye la ahí, la tierra está llamando

And the land
This land
Our land
Trembles with that familiar rhythm in response

con cun cun cun
con cun cun cun

We honor our ancestors
A blessing vouchsafed by those who bled before us
Un barrio once lost in the ways of colonialism

Materialism

Capitalism

Separatism

We march and yell poetic justice

Libertad

Pa' fuera

We Reclaim our *Tierra*

Giving hope to newborn *pitirres*
Who kiss the wind as they plant seeds of *justicia*
From valley to valley
We Reclaim

We Reclaim our *Tierra*

A neglected land
The commonwealth that made you wealth

But we don't forget
Nor will we let you forget
Where we were left

We raise the tides into monsoons
Irrigating hope
Showering in its bloom
Fertilizing the foundation of our renewal

We are reclaiming *la tierra*
So goodbye oppressors
Go
Take your tax breaks with you

Oye la ahí, la tierra está llamando

And we say —
¡Presente!
¡Pa' Lante!
¡Mi Gente!

A protest heard across the equator
A chant that binds *La Lucha*
Basta ya —
you will no longer exploit us

Oye la ahí, la tierra está llamando

Y la tierra dice

Con cun cun cun
Con cun cun cun

Can you hear us now!

This *tierra* was never for sale!

Motherland Reunification
Part I: Bertito and I

Oye, hey, Bertito, I got my flight
You got your flight?
I got my fliiiiiiiiight!!!!
Hell yeah, homie!

Oye, I was dreaming of this my entire life
But then kept waking up in this sorry-ass excuse of an American dream
It always seemed impossible to leave
But I got it... I freaking got my flight

Hey man, I was born in this sorry-ass excuse
I wasn't born in *"la Isla"*
So I don't dream of going there
But maybe one day I can

When are you leaving?
I leave tomorrow, bro
I haven't seen you all week
So let's hang for one last time before I leave

Leave to my *madre tierra*
My home, *mi Isla*, Puerto Rico
Dude, I can smell *abuelita* turning that coconut
on a wood-burning stove
Que rico, how sweet: the smell of sugar, *canela*, and *coco*

Yoooooo, I can't wait
Can't wait to hug her
Tell her how much I miss her
Tell her about this wack-ass country

How I longed to be with her
Hearing stories of *papá* when he was a good man
Before war destroyed his soul and sent us the leftovers
How I longed to be hugged by her

I hope you can come, *hermano*
I hope you can see where you come from
The many shades of our *gente*
The food, the art, the *quenepa* trees

The freaking *quenepa* trees
They're all over, yo
Everywhere

I can't wait to be with *familia* again.

Motherland Reunification
Part II: Letter One to Bertito

Dear Bertito,

The views out the window, as we were about to land, were stunning
The minute I landed everyone on the plane applauded
I got so emotional my eyes couldn't stop tearing up
Tears of joy that soon I would touch the ground of my birthplace

An emotion so overwhelming that I was paralyzed
I couldn't move for seconds, which felt like hours
Sinking deep into my chair
Wondering when I could unbuckle and run out to kiss the ground

Wondering what my *tití* looks like today
It's been fifteen years since I've seen her
Will she remember who I am?
That once, I also lived in this land

Our *tierra, hermano*

I couldn't contain myself
Pins and needles filled the in-between of my skin and muscles
My heart raced
My palms were damp

DING.....

The seat belt came off
And then I was off
Off to the baggage claim

Mentally taking snapshots of each view
I looked at as I walked through the airport

Tití was waiting for me at baggage claim
There she is
The same, as if she hadn't aged
My *tití* with her great smile and beautiful dark skin
and her Puerto Rican-red lipstick

I hope she doesn't kiss me on the forehead.

Motherland Reunification
Part III: Second Letter to Bertito

Dear Bertito,

It was everything I dreamed of and more
The weather was perfect
A familiar breeze brushed through my locs
"You are home," it whispered

The sound of the *coquís* at night guided me towards nightly bliss
Their love songs kissed my eardrums
Vibrating the most beautiful melodies
"La Isla's lullaby" my *tití* reminds me

The mornings brought back familiar scents
El café colado roasting on old iron pots
The sweet bread toasting on the press
Memories of *una Isla* you would never forget

I step outside and *el barrio dice, "¡Presente!"*
Oye, when did you arrive?
As if I was only gone for a few days, they greet
Smiles and hugs from *mi gente* who I left behind

But today I'm here, *Borinquén*
In your embrace
Bertito, I wish you could see her
I'm sure she'll remember your face

You can't deny the connection, *hermano*
Your *familia* has left their blood here

Their struggle, their triumph
Our *gente*
y en la Isla dicen — *"¡Presente!"*

Every breath brings me closer to her
I am complete here
As if everything I have gone through was washed away
And the only thing that lingered was love

It will be hard to leave again
To imagine myself anywhere else
Leaving behind parts of myself
Abuelita has my sweet coco
She just made some behind the sunrise
When *la Isla* exhales
Spreading the many scents of our *cultura* across the valleys,
the mountains, and the cities

Abuelita hugs me
And I melt in her arms
Catching a sniff of the coco that got in her hair
She squeezed and squeezed

I felt free
A spirit lifted the triggers of a past life
I wish I never left you
"You never left," *abuelita* replied.

"I held you here in my heart *desde que te fuiste, Papito.*"

And it was at that moment that I realized
No matter how far,
How much time goes by,
My beating heart reminds me why,

¡Yo te quiero, Puerto Rico!

Soy, I Am

Soy la negresa de un pueblo unido
Soy el hermano de los olvidados
Soy la promesa de los soñadores
Soy la negresa de un pueblo santo

Soy like the sun never dimming its light
Soy like *justicia,* the prophet of right
Soy la Isla that still fights to thrive

Soy el camino, la entrada y el final
Soy el sudor of those who are steadfast

on this journey,

this struggle,

this fight.

Soy el papá de los olvidados
Soy la promesa de los soñadores
Soy la negresa de un pueblo unido
Soy la negresa de un pueblo santo

¡YO SOY!

I am

Soy la gotita that exposes American lies
Soy el Taíno que jamás turned away from his tribe
Soy el jíbaro that tills the unwanted off this land
Soy la noche y el día who still serve with beaten hands
Soy el machete que libera a su gente

Soy El Grito de Lares with all yelling, "Presente"

Soy el coquí who only sings for its *pueblo*

Soy la bandera
Soy el Taíno
Soy La negresa de un pueblo unido

Struggle

My poor upbringing was not what I struggled with. My struggle was with the self. Willpower and self-doubt were my enemies at the time. I longed for a father, and most importantly a protector whom I could turn to for salvation. I had neither and felt hopeless. I flowed with the currents of the ghetto. Fighting with the self over which path to take on a daily basis. Ending up down the path of darkness since my own light was too dim to see any other option. Every moment I spent in that darkness convinced me that it was where I belonged.

I saw my community suffer. I witnessed hate in the most traumatic ways. I lived through street wars that drew new gang territories right under my feet. I ran the streets searching for a connection that I never had. A connection with a community of people that cared and protected me. That showed up; at least I thought so at the time. I witnessed friends losing mothers to cancer, losing fathers to addiction, losing themselves to the street life. I lost several of them along the way.

My mother's tears brought me back from that darkness and into a life of hope. After witnessing her suffering I decided to, at minimum, try to be a better son. That pathway was even harder than the last. My struggle was epitomized in the brutal truth: that I had a father who didn't show me any love or time, that I lived in a neighborhood that normalized drugs and violence, and that I had but myself to turn to. My mother's smile, even on days where we had nothing but cheese sandwiches for dinner, lit up the room and made us forget for a moment where we were. Instilling in us a sense of pride and hope. My struggle was not realizing it sooner.

North Philly

My North Philly was a Ghetto Oasis
Burnt orange and red bricks were our canvases

Corner bodegas, our territories
and bus stops made it easy to make that money

Empty crack vials and needles lined the alleys
Fiends in abandoned homes, stoned and unconscious,
was our reality TV,
Running when the po-po showed up, our fitness regimen,
and at night, when it truly popped off,
we would blast music out of chopped-up cars
Wit speaker-filled backs, wit no seats
Vibrating windows and girls dancing on the street

My North Philly was a Ghetto Oasis
Penny candies at sunrise
Chicken wings and *tostones* when the sun died

Abuelita yelling, "Boys, get back to school!"
and dealers pushing us young bucks to do what we knew
At the corners where street fams were built
and young bucks like us were killed

But North Philly was home
A Ghetto Oasis where street life is known

And nights get more violent
And days breed more lions

And young bucks grow older
And struggle to fight it

Survival of the fittest
North Philly can't hide it

Then drug dealing
Turn stealing
Then using, abusing

What life can I truly live
In this Ghetto Oasis?

A 90's Crime

Run, like your life depends on it
Run, don't look back
Run, he's gaining, getting closer and closer
Run, now he's yelling at me

Run, as if life saw its last day
Run, forget who you are
Run, they will never believe you
Run, so you can see another day

Run, it was just a misunderstanding
Run, it was thirty-five cents!
Run, head to the police station
Run, I'm almost there

Run, come back you spic
Run, I'll kill you spic
Run, as if life saw its last day
Run, there isn't another way

Run, he's catching up to me
Run, I'm just a kid
Run, he doesn't care
Run, I'm almost there

Run, Run, Run, Run, Run

And I ran, and ran
Ran, chased by a grown man
A man enraged
Calling me names, none of which were my own

I was just a kid
Thirteen years of life, several decades to go
So I ran
Ran as if life would see its final day

I ran and I ran
Wondering in my mind, "What did I do wrong?"
Why is this man trying to hurt me?
Why am I running for my life?

I ran
Ran for over ten blocks
Ran from hate
Ran towards safety
I ran

Officer, this man is chasing me
Officer, this spic robbed my son
Boy, come with me
Officer, I didn't do anything wrong

I ran
Ran for over ten blocks
Ran from hate
Got to the station thinking I was finally safe

I was scared
Confused
Exhausted from running
Trying to make sense of it all

They harassed me
Profiled me
Smacked, punched, shoved me in a cell
Exhausted from it all

I sat in the cell confused,
Hurt, and alone

Thirteen years old hoping they would protect me
To then be convicted by a man's hate on June 10, 1990

In the Dark

I feel like I spent my adolescent years alone
Alone, trying to figure out life
A life forced upon me
Overflowing with anger, regret, denial

A life that drives most men towards addiction
Mamá would tell me "He's still your dad no matter what"
And I hated him for not being around
At the same time cried at night missing him dearly

Wishing he could stop it all and return home
Hoping he could remember a love once held
Desiring every minute of a day spent with him
Catching a ball, drinking soda pop with *papá*

Yet here I am in the dark, trying to stop myself from feeling
Loaded with a black hole of emotion
An endless pit I continue to fill each day he's not here
Waiting for the day I can empty it all then fill it up once again

What is it all worth?
I never even had a real relationship with him
The abuser,
The drug addict,
The biological, never-present man
My *papá*, my dad

Absent to those days that *mamá* alone filled the void
Wishing he could leave it all and return home
Imagining that we can pick up where it was first felt
A *papá*'s love for his firstborn that was felt

Yet here I am in the dark, filling my heart with false hope
Desiring days of tight hugs, bedtime stories, walks to the park
Wishing
Hoping
Longing
Desperately waiting

I'll fix him, you'll see

Rehab after rehab

Hoping
Waiting
Desperately waiting

I couldn't fix him, you see

Was it me?

An endless loop of what-ifs running through my mind
Blinded by the reality that war never returned my *papá*
And *papá* never fought once to come back

Was it me?

I spent years of my adolescent life playing it over and over and over
Exhausting every possible equation, finding myself back
At the beginning,
The same outcome
In the dark, searching for the light in this life that was forced upon me

I tried everything

I saw nothing. I found nothing and, in the process, got lost in the emptiness
Beating on the door of adolescent misbehavior
Adopting the street life as my newfound savior
Running towards the stereotypes of a fatherless child

Waiting for the day I could empty it all then fill it up once again

Motherless Son

A black, damp handkerchief wipes the long day of play off your face
You look into my eyes and smile as I clean the last bit of smudge

"It was the best day ever," you tell me
I smile and remind you that tomorrow will be even better

Your face immediately turns
Getting a glimpse of the other boys leaving the playground,
Walking off, holding their mommy's hand joyfully

Your eyes beaten by the years after your mom's last breath
lock with mine

We both smile a wistful smile

We begin to walk
Holding hands
Holding on to memories of a family torn by a deadly illness
We cross the street, and you squeeze my hand
I pause

Shea butter and rose oil caught by the whiff of your inhale
I caught it too
An aroma that only we can commune with

The scent of your mother's locs
Tight curls that tickled your chest before bedtime
I can still hear your laughter in the other room
memories stored quickly, creeping into our shared space

And at that moment the anguish of my childhood rampages my heart
I can't speak

For I know too well, lonely walks
and cold beds, longing for a mother's warmth

I caress your neck as we begin to walk again
A promise that I will stay and never leave you
Relentless love and a warm bed
That only a motherless father can offer his motherless son

isawyouseeingme

I saw her as I approached my final destination.

We were both walking on the same side of the street.

She was about a thousand steps away.

Eyes wide shut and arms up
guarding the silver spoon locked away in her purse.

Body tense,

jaw squeezed,

lips contracted over her top teeth,

fingers curled back in her palms brushing against her sweat.

I saw her disappointment when she realized
that she couldn't cross in the middle of the block.

I smiled tenderly so that she would not
be threatened by my beauty.

I started to walk slowly so that she could
take the time to notice my light.

At twenty footsteps away, I smiled with my eyes,
face, mouth — hoping to disarm her loaded prejudice
and reignite the light she once walked in.

Stop, Think, Return

I return to the stage after years of suits and ties
Cubicles disguised as creative hubs wit no mics
Worker bees and workaholics struggle to get it right

Depleting the soul of a poet's inspiration
Casualties of poems causing vocabulary inflation
And I, holding on to hyperboles, searching for liberation

Water cooler chatter let loose random narratives with no arcs
My heart begs to beat again for the day I get to restart

Yet still stuck clocking in and out to 'yes sirs' and reports with no hooks

Watching my back day after day for those word crooks who I shook
Those same cats who remind me whose spot at work I took

I sparked poetic revolutions corporations can't bear to see rise

And today I return to the stage after years of suits and ties!

The Calling

HATE called again
And although
Every thought in my soul

Wanted to let it go to voicemail

My anger,
My flaws,
My lower nature,
Picked up.

"It's me. **HATE**."

"I know."

"Did you hear the verdict?"

"Yes."

"I **HATE** this America"
"I **HATE** this so-called land of the free"
"I **HATE** when people can't see me"
"I **HATE** the way American justice incarcerates me"

"Kills me."

"I **HATE**."

"I **HATE** that I have to feel **HATE**."
"Exhale **HATE**."
"Reflect **HATE**."

"I give you life,

Time."

"I **HATE** when you call
and remind me of these things."

"I **HATE** remembering."

"Feeling like we just changed owners,
still chained to the American dream,
chanting in the fields of false hope."

"I **HATE** thinking about **HATE**.
My blood rises,
stress levels push me to the brink of panic."

"Hold on."

"*LOVE* is calling."

"It's *LOVE*."

"I know."

"Then do you know you are beautiful?
A strong, passionate, loving soul,
A sweet melody on nights of cold,
A *LOVE* patiently building,
Crafting homes of *LOVE*,
Engineering foundations of solid *LOVE*."

"You are the sweet sound of kissing fish,
You are uniquely you.
A florescent brilliance that only exists in the deepest sea —
Only you can exist in the most desolate of spaces."

"You are tomorrow
And the next day gone infinite.
You are LOVE."

"But **HATE** is waiting,

Waiting!"

"I can't keep **HATE** waiting."

"Then reflect with me,
Let your bright light,
Your light of LOVE,
Illuminate the shadows of **HATE**'s existence,
Causing it to dissipate,
Vanishing in your LOVE's glow."

"For you are me,
And I will forever be you."

"**HATE** has no home here."

An American Dilemma

There's an emptiness in America's heart
This great country has lost its way
Navigating the rise of materialism as its North Star
It has forgotten that soon, we all may have to pay to stay

This great country has lost its way
Pretending that the policies created are for all
It has forgotten that soon, we all may have to pay to stay
America, whose spirit has suffered a great fall

Pretending that the policies created are for all
Is this what true democracy looks like?
America, whose spirit has suffered a great fall
It's still unjust when I'm treated unfairly under the same rights

Is this what true democracy looks like?
My feet blistered from a race that wasn't afforded a proper start
It's still unjust when I'm treated unfairly under the same rights
There's an emptiness in America's heart

I Am Sorry

Yo, yo lo siento
Mi hermano
Yo lo siento
My bro

I'm not going to tell you that it is easy
That loving unconditionally will supersede anger
That blessed days will be weighed heavier than difficult ones

Yo lo siento. I am sorry, but that is not our reality

Young ones do time for bad choices
Old ones leave home at eighteen cause they tired of double duty
And our *mamás* didn't have a *mamá*, so they did their best
And I, you, can't continue to hold any of that against any of them

They are family,
The matriarchs of our village,
The sons and daughters of our *barrio*
So I can only say, *lo siento*

I'm not going to tell you to be the bigger one
The wiser one
The have-less-in-your-cup one
No!

To embody that energy is to judge their flaws
And I can't, and will not, add that hate to my plate
So, I say I'm sorry
Yo lo siento

It will be hard, most days,
To navigate through that typhoon of family drama

But this family is all we have
This *barrio* is what we know
And they are here
Present

Engaged, with all their flaws and all their love
For me
For you
For us

I can't keep speaking ill of them
They are a part of me
As they are of you
We are them as they are us

And we bring them along with our ancestors' baggage
To the conversation

A dinner table chat turned "Eff you!" and "Who do you think you are?"
I don't need to pour gas on that flame, instead I raise my white flag
And surrender myself
Yo lo siento, with all my love

This village,
This *barrio*
Will one day rise
And together we can all stand tall

Resignation Letter to a Multimillion-Dollar Event Production Company

Dear SelfcenteredunethicaldishonestwannabepresidentCEOof unorganizedmanagement,

I regret to inform you that today will be my last day.

This past weekend's production schedule put me at nine hours of over-exhausting, unstructured, mismanaged time.

While your pockets get fatter, our guest experience suffered
Load-in and load-out were unorganized,
no one paid attention to the cad,
and plaid instead of polka dots filled the scrim,
 — although rehearsals pointed to that detail that you didn't even bother to read —
the mags went down twice,
there weren't any yellow jackets on cables running to the stage,
and guest enraged tripped over loose wires
and cluttered pedestrian pathways.
The box office was overwhelmed
because the QR codes were not scanning correctly,
and the sound bite of angry customers demanding their money back,
haunted My Sleep Last Night.

So, today I say goodbye.
Keep your AV, LED screens, and AR activation.
Blast your line array,
and rig the hell out of your own truss,
cause I'm not coming back.

I reached the max of my decibel level!

Lost Boyz 'n the Hood

Boyz 'n the hood dream
but still find it hard to shake off their frown

Mothers pray that their boyz
come home when the sun goes down

Ball courts transform from hangouts
to war zones, and young boyz yelling, "Get down"

The echoes of gunshots turn into tears and shouting from the mothers
of the Black and Brown

T-shirts are printed, memorializing those boyz
who were just hanging around

Another data point for the gun
while American politics continue to compound

Palm trees sway in the wind
and sometimes you can hear them aloud

But when palm fronds break and fall
they always remain

above

ground

A Retrospective of Regret

In retrospect, I regret nothing
The fighting
The drugs
The nightlife

Nothing

I am sorry, however, to those I hurt
Beat and embarrassed
Drugged and addicted
I am sincerely sorry

Mamá, I'm sorry I caused you pain
Sorry for the late-night calls from the police district
Walking back home in shame
Head down with only myself to blame

But I —
I regret nothing

For I, today, would not be him who only sees love, not hate
I regret not
Him who knocked on shuttered doors,
standing intoxicated on vacant lots

I regret not, *mamá*

Who would I be if my life had been lived by the rules,
rebelling against nothing?

How would I find God?
Or even acknowledge He was always watching
Through the anguish of my youth, never leaving my side

Who would I be,
If not blessed by dark dead ends that taught me to turn back?

Should I have just known before digging deeper — so deep
into the shadows of a fatherless child's grief?

All of it made me into the man I am today
So I regret nothing
Not a single day
Not a single inhale

And with every exhale, my wandering soul gets closer to God
Finding clarity on the crossroads of self-destruction
Resilient in his search for self-worth
Reborn by the covenant of the Almighty

Can I get a witness?!

My Check Didn't Bounce, I Did!

They told me that I'm too casual
That I can't present in intellectual spaces
That I can't demand the attention of the elite
That I will not have anything worth saying
That I don't belong in this circle of society
That I can't influence the influencers
That I can-not,
will not,
be, not
without their blessing,
without their acknowledgement,
without their connections,
without their ruling,
without their acceptance,
without their invitation.
I shall not speak
I shall not present
I shall not offer an opinion
I shall not be
I shall not be.

Ha, Ha, Ha, Ha…

So, I

took, I

Turned the other way and walked
I will not bow to a system that doesn't honor me
Hold space for me
See me

Accept me
Vouch for me
Believe in me
Bless me
Set me free

I will not beg to enter where I am not seen
I will not let their expensive suits and Prada glasses intimidate me
I will not come off my throne to entertain their pettiness
I will not be a part of the old boy's club
"I will not be part of it," I say!

I will not come back
Nor will I be upset
Or cry
Or regret
Or try, try again
Or give in
Or show a speck of care towards their process
Their ignorance
Their disunity
Their arrogance
Their belief
Their poor excuse for societal change
They will see me not,
¡Punto!

The Many Shades of My Ghetto

At the corner bodega, a two-inch-thick clear plexiglass wall
separates us from our humanity
The reflections on that ten-foot wall memorializes the faces
of a people just wanting to survive

But you think otherwise
Profiling us one transaction at a time
But you and I are one and the same
The shade of our skin announces our origin
Beaten by the decades of trying to reclaim
the space our ancestors bled to build

Soon after I walk in, your stare frames me, at a loss
You make no real connection
I can only see thirty different views of my innocence —
captured on the screens of your safety blanket

This America has turned my skin into a suspect

Before dialects can begin to offer a small glance
into the beauty of my people

You can't even look me in the eye

We never touch,
but I can feel your heart rate increasing as I approach the counter

We have never met,
but I can hear your memory storage sifting through profiles
of who I may be to you

You stand as I get closer
wondering if I will be that guy, or just buy

65

I can now feel the weight of your fear
Turning my sneakers into steel plates that can never lift off the ground

Now here we are

You, behind a fort that distorts the view of one another's eyes at hello
And I, relentlessly trying to face a smile that comforts you

Maybe today can be the day you see me

The child of a ghetto looking for his purpose
The father of a ghetto hoping his child returns
The brother of a ghetto watching over his siblings
The servant of a ghetto rebuilding the ghetto's perception
A man from a ghetto that shaped his integrity

Love

After twenty-four years and counting, my wife continues to be my one true love. My love poems — inspired by my life in her presence, the gaze of her eyes, her smile, and my surrender to her affection — are my most precious thoughts of her, and my love for the world. She has brought me out of the darkness of an adolescent life of trauma, a fatherless upbringing, and a rebellious posture. Every single second with her gets me closer to the man that I know I can be, the father I know my kids need, the husband my beating heart continues to mold. It is she that plants literary seeds in my mind, which then are manifested through this pen on this paper, raw and uncensored. She is my freedom, for she is what God sent when I called his name. My love poems are the breaths in between. She showed me how to love beyond my limited capacities and it is with this growth that I write about love and my journey as a seeker and servant.

Rubi wit an "i"

I met her at a bookstore
Not just any bookstore
THE bookstore
The Boricua bookstore

Taller Puertorriqueño
Our bookstore
A Phila-Ricans library of *cultura*
Colores y música

Poetry and *novelas*
That's where I met her
At the corner of the golden block
El bloque de oro

She walked in and Marc Anthony started playing in my ear
Yeah, I can build you a garden so you can lay in it all day
And we can *vivir y vivir* lo nuestro
Oooooooh weeee, she so fly

She was so so fly
Ripped jeans that flared over her docs
Peasant top rockin' the Frida look, I'm hooked
Yo, yo, yo, chilllll, she's approaching the counter

So I acted like I really didn't notice her
But she knew I was all up in her style
Counting the stitches on her hand-stitched shirt
Peeping her curls and dark skin tone

In my head I even blew her a kiss
Then the convo started like this

"Excuse me, you work here?
I would like to get information on how to volunteer."

"Umm, yeah, yeah.
Sure,
I got you.
Umm."

"You see, the lady that handles that is not here.
Why don't you give me your digits and I'll make sure we connect —
I mean, she connects with you.
I got you."

"By the way,
My name is Lucas.
And yours?"
"My name is Rubi, wit an 'i.'"

I felt as if I was twelve
and couldn't really understand what was happening to me

Couldn't tell her that we had to meet again
That I would do anything to see her again
That she was nothing I've ever had
the pleasure to be in the same room with

Yeah, she was beautiful
But there was something else
A blessing sent down from the heavens
Adorned with the purity of service and kindness

She was a Rubi
An ancient gem polished to perfection
A reflection of all that is not of this world
Standing right in front of me

My eyes couldn't stop staring
And as she walked away
My eyes escorted her every strut
Wrapped in her presence, for she was whom God sent

Love Remembrance

Que la caricia de esta noche te deje recuerdos de mi presencia
Como el olor de tu cuerpo que manchó cada pulgada de mi piel

Quiero que tus labios me extrañen profundamente
Para que el próximo beso se sienta como una reunión eterna

Deja que el viento te traiga mensajes de mi amor por ti
Refrescandote en noches calurosas susurrando, "te amo, querida"

La luna por fin despierta,
recordándote de las noches que pasamos juntos
Y hoy te digo que te amo con un anillo de matrimonio

Para que nuestros sueños se puedan realizar en este mundo
Hora por hora
Día por día
Hoy y mañana
Y cada día que siga, por todos los mundos de Dios

Love Remembrance

May the caress of this night leave you memories of my presence
Like the scent of your body that stained overy inch of my skin

I want your lips to miss me deeply
So that the next kiss feels like an everlasting reunion

Let the wind bring you messages of my love for you
Cooling you down on hot nights, whispering, "I love you, dear"

The moon finally wakes up, reminding you of the nights we spent
together
And today I tell you that I love you with a wedding ring

So that our dreams can be realized in this world
Hour by hour
Day by day
Today and tomorrow
And every day that follows, through all the worlds of God

Summer Love

Oh summer,
how I missed the days
how I loved the days
the days of warmth
drinking cold sweet tea
as you caressed my skin with your presence

in return I smile and embrace you
raise my head towards you
eyes shut, only to submit my all to you

How I loved the days

Days in which I awaken and feel you there
see you there
anticipating tomorrow's comfort
without ending today's bliss

How I miss the days

I can see the green leaves turn to brown
and I, with my head down,
begin to wonder where our time has gone
I know you will leave me soon

Oh summer, how I miss the days

When will you be back, summer?

Have you forgotten me?

Do you not know that without you,
I am forced in rooms under layers of wannabes

All who dare to be you
But can't be

All who try to bring me warmth but fall short
Cause it's you that I truly need

Oh summer, how can I begin again without you?

Friend

Back in the days I rolled thick with my clique
Getting into trouble in the light of the sun
When shadows ceased to exist
And the night showed its face
Watch your back, cat
That was the good night phrase

I grew up in the mean streets
And although the black sheep
I always had my peeps

And I remember walking these streets
Bopping our heads to dope beats
And waiting for Wu-Tang
To drop their next release

On these streets
Dope beats and your peeps
That's all you need

But when we grew older
Friends turned soldiers
Trying to survive the night
Pushing through the day without a fight

Staying out of trouble in the night of our days
Friend watching out for friend
IIow many of us truly grew up?

Ask me their names today
I remember none
Later in life I learned that true friends rise like the sun
Persistently showing up
One for all
And all for another one

And even in the darkest of days
Friends break through the darkest of clouds
Rays of light that fill each other's hearts
A constant glow that forever flows

That's my homie
That's my dude
My road dog
My friend

And without question, I show up
Because today my perspective on friends
Manifests through deeds, not rhymes

Holding space
Not the nickel nor the dime
A material escape
For expressing true emotion
Like jumping in the deep side with no expectations

Friend I am, cause you were to me
And today we can walk these streets
Knowing that tomorrow
The friend I see
Can also
Truly
See me

Mamá's Love Songs

Mamá sang *boleros*
Love songs for lovers off sync
Searching to find their way back
Boleros of verbs, nouns, and adjectives that harmonize

Mamá sang love songs
Sweet melodies of an ancient time
When love inhaled endless breaths
Bonding souls for infinite days

These are the love songs of lost lovers
Navigating them back to each other's hearts
A melodic map, true love can only decipher
A cypher composed for and by love

Mamá sang songs of love
Love songs depicting our pain
Tribulations of a journey back home
Boleros bending time towards better days

Mamá's love songs reimagined our days
Days of pain turned to love
Tattoos of love all over our souls
Scars absorbed by our beating hearts

Mamá sang *boleros*
Love songs for all, but none for her
Alone with no true love
She raised us all

With *boleros* of love.

Life

How should I begin?
Explaining why I didn't,
Couldn't, or
Kept forgetting to do that for him

Or should I say I was too busy
Watching episode after episode of pointless series?
Too busy to stop and actively listen
Ear picking up soundwaves of him crying out for help

I was rushing to get home, "I'll be back tomorrow."
Kept saying that in my head, trying to convince myself
And tomorrow became yesterday
And today I have yet to stop for a second
To be fully present

Rushing through countless days
Saw his hands raised eagerly waiting to get my attention
I flew by
Couldn't stop and immerse myself into his needs.
For once, it could have
Changed the outcome

Blinded by life's wants, not my needs,
Nor humanity's breath, how could I?
Me,
I didn't see it coming

Wasting seconds-turned-minutes
No more hours in the day

On nothing
Selfish, self-consumed
And not a day goes by that I don't think of him

So tell me, how should I begin?
Writing anecdotal memoirs of a man who couldn't do more
Caught up by ticking clocks on corner blocks
Waiting for green lights
Just so I could speed up

That dumb truck just got in front of me
Looked to the side and there he was
And I,
Driving to go nowhere
Is too overwhelming itself

If I stop now, I can't get to where I am going fast enough
So I press the gas, accelerating my life
Ignoring the surroundings of life
Rolling over speed bumps that were engineered to slow you down
and engage in humanity's life

Imagining there's nothing else in my peripheral
But my heart knew he had life
Kept playing out countless scenarios
Justifying unjust actions, time after time

It's not my fight
That's what I told myself, but I am reminded otherwise
And when I turn that corner
Not a second goes by

I can still see his hand waving
His eyes hoping to connect
"Hermanito," he yells out
In *Boricua* dialect

The daily routine of 'caught up with the hustle'
Was my excuse to forget
So tell me, how should I begin?
Not knowing if a coin,
A sandwich,
A blanket,
A hug, or an ear
Would have,
Could have kept him here,
Breaks my heart

So, now I will begin
Turning myself in
Your honor, I am guilty
It was me

So, I begin by giving voice to the voiceless we continue to ignore
Thinking our life is more valuable than theirs
Generation after generation, wanting more
But if
We
— I —
Would have slowed down

Think of life as communal prosperity
Gardens of diverse personalities
Class, gender, color — one humanity
So, your honor

I'm begging us all to begin
Make initial contact
Not let government dictate how we give back
An ancestral lineage of generations
That spoke up and woke up to reclaim and take back

Life

Just imagine the change that together we can reap
A simple hello
A smile
Acknowledge him, her
A soul who has been stripped from basic needs
And wants
Acknowledge humanity

Slow down

No more unwanted lives taken

One People (Haiku)

Standing in our light
We rise, tall as one people
Reclaiming our love

Love Letter to Papá

Papá, I know you haven't been there for me
But I still love you
I love the little time I do get to spend with you
Your bad jokes and your hugs

I love how you still ask me to buy you a beer, knowing I won't
And we both chuckle every time

I know, *papá*, that you will never stop
Never stop putting poison in your body
Never stop smoking
Never stop asking me to support your addiction

But I still love you, *papá*

I love that if you could, you would try to be a better man
I love that you let me help you at your worst
I love the times you let me cut your hair
Buy you clothes and break bread

I love that today, you tried, *papá*
Tried to be what I wanted you to be
Never once complaining about it
I love that you gave me the time

Allowed me to truly see you
See that deep down inside there's a piece of me in your heart
A piece that brings you smiles when I pull up to surprise you
I love you

And I know that you know I do
Because you love me too

I can see it in your eyes, *papá*
I can see that you would've done everything for me if you could
I can see that in you, *papá*
Someday you will see it too

A father's defeat turned into addiction and self-pity
I can't even begin to imagine your pain
A veteran's nightmare, waking up to shame
I see it in your eyes, *papá*
But you will be fine, *papá*
I know that because you had me
And I pray for you, *papá*
I pray for you, *papá*

I pray at night for you
I pray for you, *papá*
I pray
I pray
Sigo orando por ti.

Joy

Let me introduce you to Joy

One word

Such a simple word

Yet, a profound emotion I've dreamed of spending countless days in
Swim in her endless oceans
Breathe her purity
Lay in her majestic meadows
Taste the sweetness of her fruits

Spending countless days

And in her embrace, time slows down
As if nothing matters but the memory created
Per Second
Per Blink

Smile

Touch

Kiss

Each minute taking hours

Oh, how I love a long kiss
Lips caressing each crease
Taste of love's savory inflections
Inflicting reimagined passions straight into my heart

Awakened by the scent of my beloved
Intoxicated by her fragrance
The deepest breaths bring her closer
The Joy of her scent

She brings me Joy
Joy reminds me
And when I connect with the center of her eyes
I'm held captive
I can't move nor do I want to
Instead, I say

I remember Joy
And Joy reminds me
This is Joy

Still and silent
Weightless
Deep breaths inhaled only bring her closer
Sinking into loops of lost lovers
Utopia's dreamworld
Reality's archnemesis

The Joy of being with her
One with her
Kissed by her
Loved by her

Joy reminds me
This is Joy

And in her rapture is where I want to lie
Where time slows down
Ignoring the distractions
Looping through the kiss

The touch

The embrace

The beating heart

Increasing
Not wanting to reach an end
Looping right back to where it all began
Over and over

And the kiss
Oh, how I love a long kiss

You.

Me.

That was Joy.

Love Poem

This is a love poem
A hug you to death poem
An *hermanos* and sistas in protest poem
Not a division poem
A unity poem
A Herculean effort poem
I lift you up when ya down poem

This is a love poem

Amor por palabras poem

This poem is a love poem

A peace, not war poem
A shut down ICE poem
A unite *familias* poem
A shatter the wall poem
A you and I make we poem
A we and us make a new world poem

A love poem
This is a love poem
This is a love poem

A I got nothing but love for ya
Love poem
This is not a public announcement poem
Nor a clench your purse when ya see me poem
Not a shoot me poem
But embrace who I am poem

A I have a degree too poem
A I can be president poem
A love for the sake of humanity poem
A cry to all mankind that I love poem
A let's change the world with love, love poem
A it takes a *barrio* poem
A I'm that *hermano* poem

That positive, I create loving men poem
That see me serving poem
Write me a hero poem
That erase your prejudices poem
This is the love poem
The wash away all the hate in the world poem
A blessing in disguise as a Black man poem
El negrito wit talent from the hood poem

A love poem
A love poem
This is a love poem

A righteous teacher
It takes preachers
To teach ya how to love poem
A put ya weapon down, raise your love up poem
This is my love poem
A love poem

Defining Love

Love was never the four-letter word
Caught up in my throat
Knots that made me woke
To love or not to love
That was the joke

I love for what love
Walked the streets tough
Searching for myself and lots and lots and lots of love

We don't love
To love is weak
And in these streets
Love can't be seen
Nor whispered, as these cats can smell the weak

Love to love what…
Boys that matured to men
Were never shown real love
Instead shown to tough it out
Can't cry to knee scrapes
Or the belt, again, comes out

That's the tough love reflective of generational hurt,
Oppression, depression
Submission to oppressors who invaded *el corazón*
Who sold us to the highest bidder

Mamá had no chance
Papá quickly learned the dance
Get up and wipe your face

This isn't the place for tears
Can't fear them now
Can't fear them ever

And that love, how can we explain?
For love's supposed to be liberating,
Not pain

Cause Love —
Love was that thing we didn't talk about, ya dig?
You just knew how, and I had no idea

Today, we cool
But *mañana*
I can't stand the sight of you
And next week?
Holler at me tomorrow and we'll see

Bring me *pan dulce* and sweet *olores* from the kitchen
Mamá put some Love in that *arroz* and beans
Oooooh weeeee

Now that love, I carry in a special place
Laced up with days after fighting *hermanos*
Who then made up, and still was tight
Love, the love we struggle to get right
Day and night
And this love reminded me of his love
That tough love
Could never understand that love
But it was *mamá* that redefined love
Abdu'l-Bahá who reflected relentless love

Mi hijo and his love
Unfiltered love, that's pure love
Mi querida who shows up to love
For myself, who grew up with pain, not love

And *familias* torn apart from love
Oppressed we were and will still be, without love
A love that frees us to rewrite a new history of love
Preparing our shoulders for those who come next, to love

Now this is the love
I want to live, to love,
And die from

Love Letter to My First Born, Lucas Rivera III

I brought you to mind and heart during my loneliest night
It was that day I realized that *papá* could never rise to be my father

So, I thought of you
Even before I was old enough to drive
Old enough to find true love
Old enough to love and wed

Young and depleted from an unrelenting desire to mine a father's love

My father's love

Time

Presence

I thought of you

You came to me that night
And I held your hand as you took your first steps
Spoke your first words
Hit your first ball
Did your first all

I thought of you then

Calculating every second I will be spending with you
Loving you
Holding you
Guiding you

Today, you begin to make decisions on your own
Exerting freedom like a hummingbird
Navigating the wind, calculating its hovering
over the nectar of its sustenance
You will take this journey alone

Not as the third but as the first

Your light will shine
And your village, us all,
Will be illuminated.

Remembering Jesse (Haiku)

I did not lose you
Your vessel will lay in earth
Your drum still pulsates

Faith

As stated in the beginning of this book, my relationship with God was formed long before I realized what it was. My struggle as a Black and Latino man in this country brought tests and difficulties that shaped who I am today. This is the main reason I have no regrets. As hard as it may seem, I couldn't think of a life beyond this day without a relationship with God. I, however, am deeply sorry to all I have caused pain and let down. In my darkest moments, I couldn't see and therefore moved even closer to that darkness. When I met my wife, I was shown a reflection of the man I wanted to be. She reflected God through her love for me. I gravitated towards that love and, by default, gravitated towards God. When I began this journey of intentionally building a relationship with God, I understood what darkness truly was. My poems of Faith are centered around the following Bahá'í hidden word:

> **"O SON OF BEING! My love is My stronghold; he that entereth therein is safe and secure, and he that turneth away shall surely stray and perish."**
>
> **—Bahá'u'lláh**

Questions Unanswered

In this material world we continue to superficially define our existence
Our purpose
Justifying our selfish actions
Convinced that we control our destiny

Our minds continue to fog the righteous pathway created by the
Almighty
Separating itself from the spirit which provides us the light
An empty vessel left behind,
looking to be filled by the many things of this world
Navigating blindly through a road that ends nowhere

Who are we when stripped from all besides Him?

Material things have cost us nothing but pain
Suffering
War
Injustice

Who do we turn to when we awake with nothing, but in our own skin?

Hate in this world has defeated generations before us
It continues to drive those thereafter into darkness
Love for Him throughout mankind's existence
has been proven time after time to be the only remedy

How do we rise from the darkness and into the light?

When do we move towards the light?
Embracing His love with every cell
Every vein
Every follicle

Every strand of muscle
Every layer of skin
Every breath

When do we pivot, rerouting our internal compass
Calibrating our heart's gravitational pull towards love
Remembering it was darkness that clouded our joy?
The fuel of a lover's journey

My Awakening

Violence doesn't exist when I close my eyes
Closing them so tight my tears can't find escape
And when the echo of loud bangs fade
My lashes unlock the gates to the rivers of my emotions

"You're stronger than that," I tell my teenage self
Trying not to let anyone around me notice my weakness
Begging for time to speed up and return me home

But they're watching

The call of young warriors fills the corner blocks
Showcasing to each other a facade of strength
That locks away their innocence

I'm forced to stand together with my tribe
Tuning in to the strategies of revenge being spoken
Observing as the streets continue to breed vengeance
Every minute extended, creeping in my deep breaths

My facade fades slowly
Causing my chest to tighten
Heart retreating into its cavity
Contracting ever so slowly

But they're watching

The men in blue break up the chaos
Time sped up and returned me home
Alone, afraid, and exhausted I sunk into my bed
As though if I closed my eyes, tomorrow would come quickly

I couldn't fight it anymore
My mind,
body,
and soul fell

Morning breaks through the thick fog of despair
Knowing that my life, to this point, has been of my free will
At least that's what I continued to think, but didn't feel

Before I even knew who He was, God noticed me
Watching every wrong turn,
Bad choice,
Negative thought

He noticed me

The radio announces the names of the youth from last night
My eyes couldn't shut tight
My shirt got soaked
I awoke,
alone
and afraid

I kneeled
and
asked
God
to
hold
my
pain

Un Mundo/One World

Imagine *un mundo*
Where *todos* speak the language of *el arte*

Imagine *un mundo*
Where *arte* empowers *comunidad*

Imagine *un mundo*
Where *comunidad* gives birth to true *identidad*

Imagine *un mundo*
Where *identidad* reflects *colores*

Imagine *un mundo*
Where these *colores* blind Latino stereotypes

Imagine *un mundo*

One *cultura*

Un mundo
One *arte*

Un mundo
One *amor*

Un mundo
Una comunidad

One world
Un mundo

Let us reclaim

Yell

Shout

Write

Paint

Pray

Produce

Act

Protest

Run towards
Not away

Rage against negative ideas

Reflect one world

Un mundo
One culture
Una cultura

Let us unite

A More Realistic Utopia

We strive daily to find ways to differentiate ourselves from one another,
hoping that the new adjective would go viral,
or better yet, create a community of like-minded individuals
in search of just that —
community!

We all struggle to find that place of belonging.
Never once stopping to think about the disunity we are creating by
socializing a divide that only exists
after mom and pop tell us not to play with that kid,
by giving meaning and life to the unsolicited characterizations
of others we meet,
and at the same time defining classes that quickly categorizes us
within those differences.

Never once stopping to hold space for love.
Acknowledging that our differences are what make us, us.
Never once stopping to just listen.
Acknowledging that we are all connected by the same beating heart.

What if I told you that love was the only thing we needed to seed the
development of a Utopia?

A Utopia that can be realized by its protagonists.
Protagonists who reflect through deeds, not words, the meaning of love.
A love so powerful it ignites mankind's desire to serve one another.

Now imagine a community that breeds unity.
A Utopia grounded in the oneness of humanity.
Where equality is inhaled at our first breath
and inequity never found an incubator, therefore never got to exist.

Where we can all see each other as brothers and sisters,
not colors nor social divisions.
A Utopia where man stands for honesty,
truthfulness, loyalty, and
love in his journey towards establishing human equality.

Where 'woman' stands for community,
righteousness, balance, and nucleus.
The beauty of our land reflected in her melanin,
tranquility, peace, prosperity, and
love in her journey towards establishing human equality.

A Utopia where we stand for all, and none are left behind.
Bound by the laws of the land,
we stand
tilling the root cause of hate,
war,
cruelty,
selfishness.
Seeding in our hearts, the fruit of love —
love, in our journey towards cultivating an ever-advancing civilization.

A Utopia where love completes the building blocks of our DNA.
The sweetness found within the sugar group
that alternates through this chain,
and our brains, rewired, transmitting messages of service to our
hands, our feet,
our smile, our vocal cords.

And we begin with, can I get you anything else?

And you ask yourself,
How can love and its effects have such a prolific change in our world?

108

You see,
love is like a small drop of water constantly dripping on our soul.
Its consistent beat, over time, can penetrate the most negative thought
and turn it into the most powerful act of humanity.
The engineering of a Utopia powered by the matrix of its infinite love,
for eternity.

A Utopia, self-proclaimed as love's vessel, you see.
And every time you stare at the mirror
you will find it piercing your entire being.

Freeing you from the thought of false hope,
and delivering you to the beauty of who you can truly be.

If we could just surrender —
put our guard down, and just surrender —
place our bias down and just surrender —
stop waiting for tragedy to hit our community
before we all stand together —
to then surrender.

I Say Aché

Aché, aché para mi viejo padre, aché
Aché, aché para mi viejo padre, aché

You left me, at five, without a nickel or dime to my name
You blame
Mamá

But she wasn't wrong to leave

As she packed her fears and my hopes
I turned to you in tears
Can't you hear me crying?

Crying for a father, dad, *papá*
Crying for a friend, protector, *papá*
Crying for a shoulder, a hug, *papá*

Longing for you, my *papá*

Even after all these years
I am longing for you, *papá*
Even after the needles on the floor
The scabs on your arms
The unpleasant smell at your doorstep

Even after the grams of hate shot up your veins

I long for you, *papá*
Papá, I long for you

Not satisfied with just the thought
Or the desire, of fixing and having you

I need, I love, I want my *papá*

Today I say *aché*

You left me at five without a nickel or dime to my name
You blame
Mamá

You turned the other way as if we would come back
Aché for you, *papá, aché*
We never did and you never changed
Yet you blamed *mamá*

She gave us all, *papá*
She was our protector
Teacher, friend, father
No man was ever made more important than us

What you lacked
We got from her
So no more 'Yes sir' —
We now spend days and nights without the trauma of your war

Aché, aché para mi viejo padre, aché
Aché, aché para mi viejo padre, aché

I will keep you in my heart, even after all we have been through
But today I say, *aché*

Aché papá, aché
Aché, aché para mi viejo padre, aché
Aché, aché para mi viejo padre, aché

Ya Bahá'u'l-Abhá

O Thou, Glory of the All-Glorious!
I call on you
Hear my cry
See my people

I yell from the bottom of my belly
Yelling so loud that my ancestors can hear my cry
A cry out for guidance
A cry for strength

A cry for the cries of so many that I carry in my heart
A cry for the poor
The weak, the disenfranchised, the left behind,
The separated
The children
Can you hear the children cry?

I cry out for your love
A cry for our hope
A cry for this world
A cry that strips us from all save for Thee

I cry for the lost souls walking in this material world

I cry
Ya Bahá'u'l-Abhá
I yell from the bottom of my soul
Yelling so my ancestors can hear my cry

A cry for you and for me
For her and for him
For they, them, us, we,

I yell from the bottom of my soul
Ya Bahá'u'l-Abhá
I yell from the depth of my diaphragm
I yell for those that suffered before,
For the millions who will suffer after
Who can still hear my call

my cry
my love
my pain
my cry
Ya Bahá'u'l-Abhá
He gives us strengths
He gives us love
He gives us hope
He brings us joy

He brings us joy

Every day

Every hour

O Thou, Glory of the All-Glorious!

Ya Bahá'u'l-Abhá
Ya Bahá'u'l-Abhá
Ya Bahá'u'l-Abhá
Ya Bahá'u'l-Abhá

We Are Blessed

We are blessed
We are blessed because we get to build this ever-advancing civilization
A civilization grounded in love
A foundation built by the hearts of His servants
Not by the materials they posses
An ever-advancing civilization
Where women and men
Children and youth
Are all equal in His eyes

We are blessed
We are blessed because the Covenant of Bahá'u'lláh is our North Star
A North star centered on the spirit
Guided by Him who is the omnipotent

We are blessed
Blessed by the first breath we take
Awake and infused by our Faith
A Faith that begins and ends with Love
A Faith that shines even when our hearts frown
Get run down, exhausted by society's beat down
Trials and tribulations of a world that can't and won't get down
with Him

We are blessed

We are blessed

And with this blessing
We walk and serve guided by our North Star
Feet grounded by the Oneness of God

The Oneness of Religion
The Oneness of Humanity
We walk with every stride focused on the hearts of His Servants
Let deeds, not words, be your — our adorning

We are blessed

And with this blessing we are here today
We stand tall today
A physical reflection of the virtues of our Faith
We stand
Not to judge, but to hold space for love
Not to judge, but to remember His love
Not to judge, but to bring to mind — to heart, those souls
Those souls that once did all the heavy lifting
Those souls that served when the sun burned and when the rain beat
us all down
Those souls that, without request, stood at the door of true service
Adorning themselves with the jewels of His abiding service
Those souls that empty their cups daily to God and fill them up with
that which we can't handle

We are blessed

Blessed that today we are summoned to serve again
Serve the cause by engaging in prayer and bringing to mind those
lovely souls
Those souls who have the capacity to love and serve our community
The unity of a humanity brought here today by the oneness of Him

We are blessed!

A Large Voice
Inspired by Sonia Sánchez

This is a large voice
A voice that trembles the land
Infinite ripples in the oceans that unite us

This is a large voice
Painted with all the colors of the world
The darkest hue, all combined
A true reflection of us

This is an enormous voice
Chanting ancestors
Celebrating over our triumphs
A love that binds us

This is a gigantic voice
Shouting over mountain peaks
"We are one people,
One world"

This is our voice
Harmonies of warrior tribes
Preparing mankind with arrows of love
Reshaping a world lost in darkness

See our sun rising!

You're a Gift to Me

The front of you is the doorway to my soul
Intriguing the onlooker to stop and wonder what's inside
A mind, curious of letters shaped into metaphors
You remind me, I was there before

Collecting stories of adolescent misbehavior
A ghetto child's coming of age
A journey guided by the beauty of his *cultura*
Navigating through narrative arcs of rage

And then there was love, and you made me pause
Turn a glance into a days old stare
Transfixed on memories of a lover's first sight
I might stay here a bit longer

You held them all for me
I lost track of how many I was able to fit
But you kept count
Organizing it all page by page,
Section by section,
Chapter by chapter

Emotion by emotion, you illustrated it brilliantly
Captivating those who got past the cover
With love poems and hate poems,
Haikus and other forms of 'me'

I can feel every letter of 'I'
Raised on the cotton blend of 'you'
Lost in each word, hoping there's no end
You remind me I was here before

We haven't even met
And yet,
I'm thanking you for this great gift

Lifting a boy's pain
Developing each word into a man's hope
But I hope

You understand,
You will not be my one and only
You will, however, be
The first gift to me
And then there will be others

But not quite like you.

Sipping Black Beauty

I had you on a cold Friday night
My shoulders sore from a long day of carrying my skin
I closed my eyes
Began with a healing prayer

I was greeted by your Black beauty
Elated by your scent, ancient and wild
A thousand years of cultivated aromatic exquisiteness
Which only springtime can make manifest

The astringency of your body caresses the inside of my mouth
A tea of a thousand years
Your properties bring me healing
Like prayers recited by tribes when we were one land, one people

I closed my eyes again and began to sip you
My lips feel you first
Greeted by the warmth of your tenderness
I'm reminded why dynasties went to war for you

Protecting the deep roots you dug into sacred land
Not one man alone can conquer the richness of your existence
Yet here we are
Still at war by the root cause of the color of your skin

My skin

Our skin

You brought me ease
Unapologetically Black and sweet

You brought me ease
As if you felt my bones crying out for your healing
My pain simmers
The taste of you after a long day
The days only our skin can remember
Since the rest of us are still trying to get up
And stand

March

Unite

You brought me ease

And reminded me of the root cause of it all
And reminded me how we turn to the purity of your Black beauty
Again and again for healing

Ignorance Is Not Eloquent

Why don't you stop being ignorant?
Raioc your ancestral self before your mouth
Substitute the **F** in your lingo with an **L**
And let it linger a bit in your hopeful palpitations of a greater being

Let your wretchet life inspire truth
Transmute a once-lost gem in the **U** into an **O**
Omitting the facade in your wannabe persuasive front

Why don't you stop being ignorant
and bury your lower nature?

Today we raise the **V** of your virtuoso true self
Syncopating the characteristics of a beautiful soul
into an unclassified ad.

Why don't you forget about the cadence of the street front brother
and remix it into an **E**loquent poem of **LOVE**

At the End I Begin

At the end
At least the end of my first beginning
A life of struggle
Drugs
Violence
Loneliness
Abuse
Hate
Hardship
Loss
Love
And awakening

I end and begin again
A rebirth of a man eager to serve humanity with love
Exhausted by a past journey of trials
Overwhelmed by the counts of R.I.P. airbrush T-shirts I sported
And on the back shouting out
Carlito, Domingo, Green Eyes, Kiki, Tito, Joey, Flaco, Papo

And if this poem was about spitting the names of homies I lost on the
way
I would still be pushing through countless commas until I got to the
end

But instead

I'll spend this new beginning at the day where I begin again
Without regret and my heart never forgetting where I came from

I begin again

A life engineered by the remembrance of errors in my trails
My heart still beats in syncopation with those moments
But I run no more
Finding blissful days in my own skin
I run no more

Hate has no home in my soul
I remember, you told me
You showed me
So now I stand

I stand at this beginning with my head bowing to the east
Raising to the west
The cycle of a day in blessings and services
In prayer guided by the Omnipotent, the All-Wise

I rise in an understanding that hope brought me here
That the light of that hope guided me here
That I'm here, *¡Presente!*

And for my *gente*
I offer you this —
I
Could
Never
Have
Developed
to
Whom
I

Became
Without
Our
Pain

Your
Love

Your
Hope

Supporting
The
Hours
I
Spent
Getting
It
Wrong
Never
Once
Judging
But
Insisting
To
Try
Again
Pushing
Me
To
Try
Again
Never

Turning
Your
Back
As
If
God
Told
You
I
Was
Worth
Saving
I
Begin
Again
For
You

For the new generation that's stuck trying to find themselves
For the old generation that's stuck trying to let go of their old selves
For the future generation that's hungry
I begin again at the end of my first beginning
To stand in my light
Rise in my hope
Begin a new day that's fueled by the DNA of love warriors
On the battlefield, opposite of hate
Heart wide open to embrace those that can't find another way

I stand
With deeds, not words
Relentlessly navigating and negotiating a material world
Like a hummingbird, sharp and gentle,
Staccato and yet focused,
Feeding its soul with the nourishment of this land

I stand

At an end that's no longer familiar

A fresh scent of aspirations inspired by desires to be a better man

Awakened from the darkest of days by a single light

A light that guided me here

To this new day

This new moment in time

For you and those that will come after.

Taíno Petroglyphs

Identidad

El Coquí is a tiny brown frog native to *la Isla de* Puerto Rico.

Struggle

The spiral represents cosmic energy and unendingness, it also signifies the journey and change of life as it unfolds.

Love

The *Taíno* symbol for heart where the beating drum of love is manifested.

Faith

The God Sun. *Taínos* believe it is the source of life and good favors.

About the Author

Lucas Rivera is a multidisciplinary Afro-Puerto Rican artist and innovative arts and entertainment management executive with over twenty years of senior leadership experience. He has a track record of success in marketing, program development, strategy development, talent relations, nonprofit management, and event planning.

Born in Salinas, Puerto Rico in 1977, Rivera built his professional arts career serving his Latino community in North Philadelphia for more than sixteen years. He spearheaded the development and implementation of a new arts facility focused on arts education for high school students at Esperanza Academy Charter. He then became the Executive Director of Artist and Musicians of Latin America, AMLA, where he produce community centered salsa festivals and helped develop the next generation of Latin Jazz artists in that community.

Rivera made a name for himself in LA as the visionary behind Grand Park, a new Los Angeles County Park in Downtown Los Angeles operated by The Music Center. He then joined Fairplex as Senior Vice President of Marketing and Programming, where he helped usher in a new era of creating events that celebrate the City of Pomona and Southern California's cultural diversity. Currently, Rivera is the Founder and CEO of Sakul Creative, a consulting agency that focuses on event strategy and program development grounded in community.

Printed in the USA
CPSIA information can be obtained
at www.ICGtesting.com
BVHW031931300823
668989BV00004B/22